George Mahood

CHASING TRAILS
A Short Fun Book about a Long Miserable Run
(The prequel to the DNF Series)

Copyright © 2021 by George Mahood

All rights reserved. This book or any portion thereof may not be reproduced or used in any manner whatsoever without the express written permission of the author except for the use of brief quotations in a book review.

This edition published 2021 by George Mahood.

www.facebook.com/georgemahood
www.instagram.com/georgemahood
www.twitter.com/georgemahood
www.georgemahood.com

ONE

'One, two, three, GO!' I shouted, clutching my backpack straps tightly and running towards the top of the downslope. I took an enormous leap forward, swinging both legs in front of me, and landed in a seated position. I was already travelling at considerable speed before I hit the muddy ground, and it only took a few seconds to reach what felt like terminal velocity. My shorts were sucked right up my bum crack, making it feel like I was sledging in a thong. But it was so much better than sledging. Who needs snow? Or a sledge? This was the most fun I'd had in ages.

I must have travelled well over 50 metres before I heard a suspicious tearing noise from my shorts. Very few things could make running 36 miles in the conditions we had faced less appealing, but doing so with a pair of shredded shorts – and no underwear – would be a step too far. I tried in vain to dig my heels into the ground to slow myself down and used the fingers on my right hand to scrape into the grass. My left hand was still sore after my fall earlier in the day, but I had temporarily forgotten about it until I was hurtling down a muddy hillside on my backside, unable to stop. When my friend Mark had suggested to me that we take part in an ultramarathon together, this was not quite what I had envisaged.

When I hung up the phone after Mark had tried to convince me that the two of us were going to run an ultramarathon together, I didn't think there was any chance it would ever happen. An ultramarathon is any run further than a standard 26.2-mile marathon. I had absolutely no desire to run one. I tried many times over the years to learn how to love running, but running and I just never clicked. It always hurt. It was always tiring. It was always boring. Extending this misery for a longer period, and over more difficult terrain, seemed completely illogical. Ultrarunning was for crazy people.

But I had said that about an Ironman, too. And yet I had recently taken part in my first Ironman; something that was not even a pipedream until I was lying in a hospital bed four months previously, having had surgery to remove a spinal cord tumour (see my book Operation Ironman: One Man's Four Month Journey from Hospital Bed to Ironman Triathlon). I do wonder if they perhaps removed a part of my brain by mistake in that operating theatre. Because as much as I despised the idea of ultrarunning, I became equally intrigued by the prospect over the weeks following that phone conversation with Mark.

I started reading more about ultramarathons and the idea slowly grew on me. Perhaps these ultras were not so bad after all. They sounded very different from normal road races; you tend to run at a much slower pace; it's usually over varying terrain (often on trails); and eating lots of food throughout is essential. It's basically a long and miserable picnic.

The word 'trail' conjures up images of somewhere wild, faraway and exotic; a track made by early explorers perhaps – or maybe just animals – full of mystery and intrigue. It is very much an American word. In Britain, we just use the word 'footpath'. A footpath, on the other hand, conjures up images of a well-trodden, well signposted route, frequented by elderly dog-walkers. Which is what most trails are, too. But trails sound way cooler.

The term 'trail running' used to annoy me immensely. It has gained popularity in recent years in the UK, but if I ever heard people talking about going 'trail running' I used to think, 'oh, right, you mean you're going to run along a footpath?' But I eventually warmed to the name when I realised I would much rather be a trail runner than a footpath runner.

After reading so much about trail running, I thought I should give it a try to see what all the fuss was about. It wasn't long before I embraced it. Instead of going out for a run along the roads – as I would occasionally do, to try to keep fit – I picked routes along footpaths, sorry I mean trails. It took me a little while to get used to the different technique and sensations with off-road running, but I realised it was far more enjoyable than running on tarmac. Trail running seemed to solve all the problems that I had with running. It didn't seem to hurt as much – because varying your stride with the changing terrain helps prevent repetitive overuse of the same muscles; it wasn't nearly as tiring because my pace was considerably slower;

and if a section was especially steep, or muddy, or rocky (or, more often than not, all three) then I just walked. And, because of the varying landscape, and having to pay close attention to my footing, it was certainly never boring.

It was in late November, as I was searching online for possible events, that I stumbled upon the EnduranceLife South Devon Coastal Ultra. It seemed to fit the bill perfectly. The race took place in early February, which would allow very little time to train (I saw this as a positive, as I didn't want too much time to get anxious or obsessive about my preparation). It was relatively close to home, giving it the added appeal of convenience. And it was 'only' 36 miles. 36 miles is a very long way, but it is a lot shorter than many ultras, so I figured if I was going to subject myself to an ultramarathon, then the South Devon Coastal was probably as good as it was going to get.

Mark was delighted that I was up for the challenge. We both signed up to the event and he booked his train ticket to come and stay with us in Devon in early February.

TWO

I have completed a few marathons over the years, and after each one I have crossed the finish line genuinely feeling that if the race had been even half-a-mile longer, I would not have been able to finish it. So how on earth would I be able to run 36 miles?

I also knew that I felt the same when I used to take part in parkrun when we lived in Northampton (parkrun – for those that don't know – is a series of timed 5k running events that take place in towns and cities around the world, usually at 9am on Saturday mornings. They are completely free and encompass all ages and abilities. If you've never been, and like the idea of getting into running, I would highly recommend it. Find your local one here... www.parkrun.com). I used to cross the finish line of those 5k races, feeling that if the race had been even 10 metres longer, I would not have been able to complete it. When running, your body and mind seem to adapt to the distance that you have set yourself. A marathon is not the same as running a half marathon and then running another half marathon. Yes, mathematically it is, but psychologically it is very different. A marathon is just the same as a half marathon, or a 10k, or a 5k parkrun, except the start line and finish lines are further apart. I hoped it would be the same with an ultramarathon.

While researching the race, I found a blog post about the Sound Devon Coastal that included a mention of a runner named James Adams. James Adams writes a popular running blog called Running and Stuff, which is about running... and stuff. He is a hugely experienced ultrarunner and has taken part in many of the longest and most gruelling running races in the world, including: the Marathon des Sables (146 miles over several days across the Sahara Desert), the Spartathlon (153 mile continuous race in Greece), the GUCR (145 miles along the Grand Union Canal), the Badwater Ultramarathon (135 mile run starting at Death Valley in 50°C heat), and then a 3,200 mile run across America (a 3,200 mile run across America). There aren't many runners out there with a more impressive CV.

I was curious to know how someone with such vast experience and familiarity with pain and suffering would fare with the relative ease of a measly 36 mile run in south west England. He may not be the fastest of runners, but his experience would shine through and surely he would have been up there amongst the top finishers. I found the results online for the year he took part and slowly scrolled down the list of 100 competitors looking for James Adams' name. Not in the top 10? Oh well, he doesn't claim to be fast. Not in the top 50? Perhaps he was just taking it easy. Not in the top 80? He must have had an off day. I reached the end of the list of the 100 finishers and there was no mention of James Adams. I scrolled back to the top and came slowly down again. Still no sign. Perhaps he ran under a pseudonym, like some sort of superhero? Or maybe James Adams was his online cover name, to protect him from freaky stalkers (like me)? I reached the end of the list again and then noticed a bunch of other names at the bottom of the spreadsheet without a time recorded. Amongst them, James Adams, and next to it, the three letters that haunt all competitors: DNF. Did Not Finish.

I phoned Mark. Mark had first alerted me to James Adams' blog a few months previously and was a big fan.

'Did you know James Adams took part in the South Devon Coastal a few years ago?'

'Did he? How did he get on?'

'He DNF'd.'

'Ha! Yeah right.'

'He did.'

'Seriously?'

'Yes. I've got the race results here in front of me.'

'But surely that would have been a walk in the park compared to what he's done?'

'That's what I thought.'

'Oh shit. What the hell have we signed up for?'

'I wish I'd googled it before we paid our entry fee.'

'Oh well. It's a bit late for that now.'

I began to panic. We were completely out of our depth. Perhaps it was 'only' a measly 36 miles for a reason.

I did some further research and eventually found a very short race report that Adams had written about his participation in the South Devon Coastal Ultra. I was relieved to discover that he took part in the race during his stag weekend. As you would. He was hung-over, possibly drunk, and after he made it to the end of the first loop, with another seven miles remaining, the lure of the pub and his friends all eating fish and chips was too much, so he decided to stop. And who could blame him?

The UK had been suffering from the wettest winter since records began. It felt like it had rained non-stop for months. In some parts of the UK, it genuinely had. The village of Eglwyswrw (bless you) in Pembrokeshire recorded rain for 85 consecutive days, ending on 21st January, just a couple of weeks before our run. It was five days short of the UK record set in 1923.

THREE

The weather deteriorated further during the week before the race, and the forecast for race day got progressively worse each time I checked. By the time I picked Mark up from the train station the day before the run, a 'severe weather warning' had been issued and we faced the prospect of 60mph wind and heavy rain from morning until night. We ate a gigantic bowl of pasta for dinner and went to bed early with a glimmer of hope that the whole thing might get cancelled before we even had to leave the comfort of the house.

Waking at 5am is never fun. Waking at 5am with a stinking cold as the rain and wind batter the window and the realisation hits you that today is the day that you have stupidly signed up to take part in an ultramarathon along some of the toughest terrain in the UK, is as far from fun as it is possible to get.

I crawled out of bed and picked up the pile of clothes I had left out the night before, closed the bedroom door quietly so as not to wake my wife, Rachel – who is even less of a morning person than I am – and made my way downstairs where I met Mark in the kitchen. We acknowledged each other with a nod. No words were needed.

I switched on the kettle and put some bread in the toaster. I really didn't feel like eating, but knew I needed to have some breakfast to help prepare myself for the day ahead.

I had woken several times during the night and each time checked the race organiser's website and Facebook page on my phone, secretly hoping there would be an announcement cancelling the race because of the extreme conditions. I half-heartedly checked again as I waited for the kettle to boil.

'Any updates?' asked Mark, knowing instinctively that I was looking for a message about the race.

'Yes,' I said, as I hurriedly read a new post that had appeared on the event website. 'It says here that due to extreme weather conditions, the route may have to be amended slightly and will continue to be monitored throughout the day. It also implies that they might still cancel it before we even start.'

'I can't decide if it would be better to be cancelled completely or drastically rerouted.'

'Me neither. It would be a bit annoying if the race goes ahead, but ends up being 500 laps around the registration marquee instead.'

'Well, at least that would be dry.'

'Good point. And flat and out of the wind. Actually, I'd definitely be up for that.'

I spread some peanut butter and jam thickly onto the toast and handed a piece to Mark.

'Pork pie?' I said, offering one to Mark.

'For breakfast? No thanks.'

'No, to take with us. I'm going to pack one in my backpack.'

'Go on then. Thanks.'

'Mustard?'

'Really?'

'Of course. A pork pie is not the same without mustard.'

'That's true. Are you planning on carrying a whole jar of mustard with you?'

'I was going to, but I had a brilliant idea in the middle of the night.'

'You were thinking about pork pies in the middle of the night?'

'Yes, of course. Don't you?'

'Actually, yeah, I sometimes do.'

'Watch this!'

I took a sharp knife and sliced the pork pie in half through the middle like a bread roll - horizontally, rather than vertically. I then spread a large quantity of English mustard onto one half and sandwiched the two pieces back together.'

'That's genius,' said Mark.

'I know. It had been bothering me for ages about what to do. Cornish pasty?'

'Are you serious?'

'Yes, I bought them specially. I relied on a diet of pasties for most of my Ironman training.'

'Why not! Thanks.'

Surviving the ultramarathon would be all about eating. I don't know much (anything) about sports nutrition, but I read somewhere that the human body only stores enough energy to allow for about 90 minutes of strenuous exercise. In order for these energy stores to be replenished, you need to eat and drink regularly. There are hundreds of books and articles about the best foods to eat, many of them contradicting each other, so it makes planning the food for an endurance event quite complicated. I solved this problem by filling my backpack with lots of everything: cereal bars, energy gels, flapjack, nuts and raisins, chocolate, sandwiches and, of course, a huge pork pie and a steak pasty. Mark had much simpler dietary needs. His backpack was filled with eight peanut butter and jam sandwiches, plus the pork pie and the pasty.

They had also issued us a mandatory kit list of things we must carry with us at all times. This included: a mobile phone, food, water, head-torch, money, jacket, foil blanket, whistle, first aid kit and a hat. Fitting everything in our backpacks was its very own endurance challenge.

We reluctantly drove over to the start of the race in the small village of Beesands on the South Devon coast. It was early February, 6am, pitch black and unbelievably miserable outside. Beesands had staged the event for several years and used to have a long, large, well-surfaced car park that stretched the entire length of the seafront.

Two years previously, a series of severe storms washed this car park away completely. Most of it is now several miles up the coast near Dartmouth. And underwater. Which makes it a little impractical to park on. Undeterred, and keen to keep the race start where it had traditionally been, the race organisers instead asked runners to park in a village three miles away where a shuttle bus would be provided to take them to the start.

They also said that there would be some limited parking available in Beesands for the extremely early ultrarunners. There were fewer than 100 people taking part in the Ultra, but hundreds more would take part in the marathon, half-marathon and 10k events, which would all take place at staggered intervals later the same day. We hoped that we would be early enough to be one of the privileged few to be allowed to park in the village. It wasn't so much the idea of getting the bus to the start that didn't appeal, rather the wait to get one back at the end of the day. We were likely to be amongst the last of finishers – if we finished – and I had a fear of the marshals and the bus drivers buggering off home and leaving us stranded in the middle of nowhere.

A man in a large orange high-vis coat stuck out an arm to signal us to stop as we pulled into the village.

'Oh, here we go,' I said to Mark. 'Is he going to make us turn around and drive back to wait for the shuttle bus?'

'Morning lads,' he said, leaning in through my window so far that I thought he was actually going to climb in and join us. The rain ran down the hood of his coat and dribbled onto my leg. 'Thanks for braving it here, despite these conditions.'

'Thank you for braving it, too,' I said. 'At least we are inside a warm car.'

'Yes, you are,' he said. 'For now. I don't envy you for the conditions you'll be running in today.'

'Don't remind us,' said Mark.

'If you drive down here and turn left at the bottom, you'll see another man dressed like me who will show you where to park. Have a good day.'

'Thank you. You too.'

As we parked the car at the end of an unlit side road and turned off the engine, the car began rocking from side to side in the wind. A horizontal deluge of rain was visible in the headlights of the other cars as they parked up alongside us.

'Running along the coast path can't be possible in this weather?' I said.

'Maybe it will brighten up,' said Mark optimistically, as we gazed out onto what looked like the end of the world.

I had brought a flask of coffee with us and we sat in silence in the darkness for about twenty minutes, delaying the inevitable fact that we were going to have to venture out of the car at some point.

FOUR

The race HQ was situated in a soggy field, a five-minute walk from the car. We made our way there, still half expecting (and perhaps hoping) that the race would be called off. Cars were backed up along the road coming down into Beesands and we felt relieved that we had at least been able to get a parking space. It was a small comfort.

EnduranceLife began as a small company set up by a group of friends in Devon in 2003. I took part in the half marathon in Beesands during one of its first few years. At the time, the race HQ consisted of a small lone gazebo outside the pub. The company has since grown considerably, staging many races nationwide and has developed a reputation of being one of the most prominent organisers of endurance events in the UK. Nowadays, the race HQ involves two huge marquees occupying a field behind the pub.

But despite the marquees and the reputation, there was nothing they could do to match the power of the British weather. As we queued up to register, we were already ankle-deep in mud, inside the marquee. Things didn't bode well for the rest of the day. One of the event staff handed us a waiver, which I obviously didn't read, but it probably explained that there was a very high likelihood of death and that we had foolishly paid money to be there and so it would serve us goddamn right if we decided to go ahead and take part anyway. We signed the piece of paper.

They then gave us a very nice orange souvenir t-shirt. It is always dangerous being given the race memento before the event. The temptation was to hotfoot it back to the warmth of the car and head home with a nice new t-shirt, without even having to suffer. We considered this momentarily, but then I unfolded the t-shirt and saw it was emblazoned with three words: NEVER GIVE UP. Oh bollocks! There goes that plan. Retreating to the car before the race had started would not really be in keeping with the ethos of endurance events.

All ultrarunners were called through into the adjacent marquee, where we would be given our race briefing. There were murmurings going around those assembled that they might announce that they were cancelling the race, or perhaps cutting it dramatically short.

As we stood waiting for the briefing, I turned and spotted some friends of mine, Daniel, Marta, and Charles. Daniel and Marta are a Spanish couple who moved over to Devon with their three children two years previously. They drove around the country with their caravan and reached South Devon, decided it looked like a nice place to live, so moved over from Spain a few weeks later. Daniel and Marta are both extremely athletic and have taken part in many triathlons and endurance events all over the world. They always train together and wear matching his and hers running and cycling outfits.

Charles is a South African who has lived in England for the past ten years. He had recently been made redundant and had filled his time between applying for jobs and attending interviews with running. Lots of running. He was noticeably fitter than me and liked to remind me of this at regular intervals.

When we moved to Devon, I didn't imagine that my attempts to make friends and integrate with the locals would involve me spending my time running with two Spaniards and a South African.

Daniel and Marta were as upbeat and enthusiastic as ever, and Charles stood there shivering despite wearing enough clothing for an expedition to the Arctic – his South African blood still not conditioned to the British weather even after ten years. They were also accompanied by Ricard – Daniel and Marta's energetic and charismatic friend, who was over from Barcelona for the weekend especially for this race. I had met him only briefly on the school run the day before. Ricard is a phenomenal runner and had high hopes of leaving England with a medal. But on the morning of the ultramarathon he looked a shell of himself. He stood there, his head hung low, and I could hear him sighing deeply to himself.

Daniel spotted me looking at Ricard with concern.

'Ricard iz not good,' he said.

'Is he ill?' I asked.

'No. He doesn't like zis weather. He az been thinking maybe he might not even start zee race.'

'But he's come all the way over from Barcelona to take part.'

'I know, that's what I tell him. He thinks it eez stupid running in zees conditions.'

'Well, I suppose he has a point.'

'Of course he does. But I don't want to say theez to him.'

There was a crackle of a microphone and one of the race organisers' voices spoke in intermittent bursts over the bustle of the assembled runners.

'WE CAN'T HEAR YOU!' shouted a man to my right.

The race organiser tapped the microphone and tried again.

'Test... test... one... three,' it stuttered.

The wet weather had taken its first casualty of the day. The man left the marquee and returned five minutes later with a new microphone, plugged it in and we could finally hear him. Despite the rumours, the race briefing made no mention of any cancellation or even any route changes. He reminded us to take extra care because of the weather, but it miraculously seemed to be going ahead as planned.

I looked back and saw Ricard with his head in his hands, regretting his stupid decision to board a flight from sunny Barcelona to the storm-battered south west coast of Great Britain. Mark and I smiled at each other. Ricard's misery at least made us seem relatively euphoric in comparison.

Stepping into a portable toilet is never normally a pleasant experience, but, after venturing through the mud across the field in the wind and rain, the sheltered and surprisingly clean interior of the toilet felt like a haven. I sat there for a while, putting off returning to the wild weather outside. As I sat there, I was disturbed by an almighty banging on the door and the cubicle shook violently.

'Just a minute!' I shouted.

There was a brief pause and then the banging and the shaking started again, this time with slightly more anger.

'OK! I'll be right out!'

It was at this point that I realised that the brutal force trying to shake me from the cubicle was actually the wind. My day was looking fairly bleak already, but the prospect of being trapped in an upturned toilet as the contents spewed over my helpless body did not appeal, so I hastily escaped from the cubicle before the wind had its way. The following morning, a photo was posted on EnduranceLife's Facebook page of one of these very toilets lying on its side.

'Where have you been?' asked Mark, with slight concern on his face. 'The race is about to start.'

'Sorry, I was just having a bit of a moment on the toilet. I'm fine now though.'

The assembled ultrarunners gathered in the middle of the field near to the start line. Mark and I were busy taking a selfie when the race hooter sounded, but we were right at the very back of the pack, so it didn't matter. We had earlier said goodbye to Daniel, Marta, Charles and Ricard, and, as the runners all headed diagonally up a steep grassy field, I could see them all disappearing off ahead. It was extremely unlikely we would see any of them again during the race, and I had told them not to wait around at the end for us to finish. We arranged to meet at the pub later that evening for beer and pizza instead.

We passed through a gate at the top of the field and then had to descend diagonally down across the next field to the bottom corner. It was at this point I realised just how slippery it was underfoot. Each time we tried to plant a foot onto the sodden hillside, our feet slid from underneath us. We had been running for less than two minutes when I saw my first faller – a man just in front of me slipping spectacularly and coating every inch of his legs, buttocks and back with mud. Then another runner went down. And then another. I came very close several times during this early section, but somehow stayed upright. But I knew my time would come. Little did I realise that this would be one of the easiest sections of the entire day, and we still had a little less than 36 miles to go.

As we made our way down to the South West Coast Path, the sea emerged through the mist, thrashing angrily below us on our left. The rain had eased slightly since the start and I didn't feel too cold. Perhaps the day was going to be ok after all.

FIVE

I have been best friends with Mark since I was eight years old. We went to primary school together, then secondary school. We played for the same football team as children, then again as adults. We played in a band together for many years and went to universities fifty miles apart. After university, we spent a few months driving across America together (see my book Not Tonight, Josephine: A Road Trip Through Small Town America), and Mark was bestman at my wedding alongside my other friend Damo (who claims his grandma invented banoffee pie).

Mark is an experienced ultrarunner. Or so I kept telling him. And everyone I introduced him to. Mark had, in fact, competed in one ultramarathon. And it is considered to be one of the shortest ultramarathons in the world. An ultramarathon is defined as any run longer than 26.2 miles. Mark took part in the Three Forts Challenge, which is a distance of 27 miles. Still, in my eyes, he was an experienced ultrarunner.

'But you've competed in an Ironman,' he argued.

'So?'

'That's doing physical activity all day. The longest physical activity I've ever done is about five hours.'

'The Ironman was different. Nearly half of that time I was sitting on my bike. I've never run a metre over 26.2 miles. You're definitely the favourite.'

'Favourite? Whatever.'

Variations of this pointless argument began every time I spoke to Mark in the buildup to the ultramarathon. We both tried to convince each other that we were the inferior runner, and that during the ultramarathon the onus would be on one of us to drag the other round. The truth is, we were both probably evenly matched. Mark was much fitter and quicker at running than me, but also had a tendency to go off way too quickly and then suffering later. I am slow and steady, and taking part in an Ironman probably helped condition me slightly to be able to keep plodding on for many hours. We would hopefully make a great team.

Just south of the village of Beesands lies Hallsands – a once thriving fishing village perched in a precarious position by the sea. In 1891, the village had a population of 159 and comprised 37 houses and a pub. Over the following years, the rising tides caused the sea wall to be breached several times, and by the end of 1917, only one house remained habitable. It used to be possible to walk around the deserted village, but now visitors are restricted to a viewing platform, as the remaining buildings are extremely unsafe.

The path led down to the beach at Hallsands, which is now made mostly of peat, as the shingle had also recently washed away. We ran along the beach for a short section, before navigating a wide stream that spread itself across the beach as it funnelled down towards the sea. A few stepping-stones crossed part of it, and we hopped clumsily from one to the other, before realising that there was little point putting off the inevitable. Our feet would not be staying dry today. I plunged my feet into the icy ankle-deep water, and, after the initial shock, it was a relief knowing that I no longer had to make any attempt to try to keep my shoes dry.

From Hallsands, the coast path climbed steadily towards the dramatic outcrop of Start Point that loomed ominously in the distance. Through the early morning haze, we could see the intermittent flashes from Start Point lighthouse as we progressed out onto the peninsula, the sea dropping further below us down to our left. The fields continued to rise upwards to our right too, protecting us from the worst of the weather.

'It's nowhere near as bad as I thought it would be,' I shouted to Mark, who was a couple of strides ahead of me.

'No. This is quite nice. Hopefully, it will be like this all day,' he said.

After a section of deep slimy mud that required some considerable squelching, we reached the car park at Start Point and then followed the luxury of a stretch of tarmacked road that meandered down to the lighthouse. It was a spectacular setting for a run. Mark and I were loving every minute.

This enthusiasm was short-lived, however. Just before reaching the lighthouse, the coast path turned away from the road and we climbed up and over the rocky headland. We had been unaware of just how much this headland had been protecting us from the wind. As we crested the ridge, the force of it almost sent us back the way we had come. Mark turned and shouted something to me. At least, his lips moved, and his face gave the impression that he was shouting, but I couldn't hear anything that came out of his mouth. I am fairly certain it was an obscenity about the dramatic change in weather, so I mouthed one back to him and we ducked our heads and pushed onward.

This peninsula marked the point on the course where we would stop running south and begin heading west. We would run west, into this wind, for about nine miles, all the way to the shores of the Kingsbridge estuary.

The wind was ferocious, and now, with precipitous drops to our left, we needed to take extra care along the narrow coast path. We were towards the back of the pack, so there was not too much of an issue with runners overtaking us, and certainly no possibility of us needing to overtake other runners.

SIX

We had covered about three miles when we came around a corner and saw what must have been one of the most miserable spots in the world to be an event photographer. The poor man or woman (their head was wrapped up so tightly I can't even be sure it was a human) had his or her face squashed up to the viewfinder and the long telephoto lens of the camera pointed at the oncoming runners. Not only did they have to lean back into the wind to try to remain in a seated position, but the camera lens was visibly twisting away from the action because of the force of the weather. They had to fight to keep the camera even remotely steady. Despite the horrendous conditions, I knew I would rather be running than sitting there. The company responsible for making a short film about the event posted the following message on Facebook the next day: 'Capturing our planned shot list proved near impossible. Incredibly harsh conditions for all involved – not least our new movie camera, which paid the ultimate price'.

We had been going for almost an hour when we saw a runner ahead, standing to one side of the path to allow us to pass. As we got closer, we realised it was Ricard – Daniel and Marta's Spanish friend. He looked even more miserable than he had at the start of the race.

'Hey Ricard!' I said. 'How are you?'

'Not good,' he said. 'Not good at all.'

'What's up?'

'I've fallen over six times. My back hurts, my legs hurt. I've had enough. I'm going home.'

'To Barcelona?'

'Well, yes, tomorrow. But now I go back to where we started the race.'

'Really? But you came all the way over here, especially for this.'

'Yes, but I don't want to do any more. And this weather.... It's so annoying. Arghhh!' he shouted, which is Spanish for 'Arghhh.'

'How will you get back?'

'Walk. The same way I ran.'

'I'm sorry to hear that. Take care. Will you still come to the pub later?'

'Of course,' he said.

It took Ricard three hours to walk back to the start, but when we saw him in the pub later that night, he was a much happier man. He didn't seem to still be suffering from any of his injuries, and it seemed that perhaps it was his pride – after the realisation that he would not be a podium contender – that had suffered the biggest dent.

I had my first fall shortly after passing Ricard. My legs went from under me on a grassy downhill section, and I landed on my backside.

'Are you ok?' shouted Mark. Or at least, I think that's what he shouted.

'Yep, fine thanks. It was going to happen sooner or later.'

My next one happened a lot sooner than I hoped. Just a few hundred metres further on, I did the same thing. This time I got back to my feet before Mark noticed and quickly caught him up and acted as if nothing had happened.

We had been running for about nine miles when a young runner passed us. He skipped effortlessly along the coast path like a mountain goat. I mean, in the sense that he seemed at one with the terrain. He wasn't on all fours. We then realised that he was the lead runner from the marathon race, which had started half an hour after ours. Over the next few miles, a steady stream of marathon runners passed us. The speed at which they navigated the treacherous rocky terrain was astonishing and quite scary to witness. We offered our encouragement to each runner who passed us, and they did the same back to us. There was a lot of mutual respect shared between runners; we were in awe of them being able to cover the same ground as us, at a far quicker pace, and they admired us for signing up to the longer distance.

The wind was relentless. As if to illustrate just how windy it was, nature gave us a unique demonstration. As we ran along the high cliff top above Elender Cove, we could see a stream running down the valley ahead of us to where it would usually topple over the cliff edge to form a waterfall onto the rocks on the beach way below. But not today. As the water from the stream flowed over the edge to begin its free fall, the continuous barrage of wind from underneath sent all the water skyward. The jet of water was propelled into the air, defying gravity like a geyser, before being dispersed as mist by the wind. It was astonishing to watch and then exhilarating to run through.

SEVEN

'How long have we been running?' I asked Mark.

'Either one or two hours and thirty-eight minutes.'

'What do you mean one OR two hours?'

'Well, it's definitely more than 38 minutes, but less than 3 hours and 38 minutes.'

'I don't understand. What are you talking about?'

'My stopwatch doesn't record hours, remember?'

'Oh my god! Do you really still have that same stupid watch?'

'It's not a stupid watch. It does the job just fine.'

I don't know how it had slipped my mind, but Mark owns quite possibly the stupidest stopwatch in the world. It is a normal looking digital sports watch, but it has, what I consider, a fairly major design flaw. The stopwatch function on the watch does not record hours. It gets to 59 minutes and 59 seconds and then starts again from zero. It is not broken. Hours are just not one of its functions. There is not even a space on the watch's LCD display where the hour unit could go. It seems to me that the hour is quite an important measurement of time. Surely it should be a prerequisite that a stopwatch should record hours?

When Mark and I first started running together back in Northampton, it was never a concern. Our runs were rarely longer than 30 minutes, and we certainly never ventured out for longer than an hour. His watch's limitations came to light when we did our first long run together while training for a marathon. It amused me greatly.

'It was cheap!' argued Mark when I questioned him about it.

'So? Even the cheapest stopwatch I've ever seen records hours. I doubt the manufacturer decided to save money by not including hours on the LCD display.'

'Why else would they?'

'I DON'T KNOW! That's why it's such a stupid watch.'

'Well, why didn't you bring your own watch? At least I've got a watch.'

'Because I saw you had a watch. If I'd known it was THAT watch, then I would have obviously brought one.'

'I've got an idea. We can just hold up our fingers every time it reaches an hour. I'm fairly sure we've only been going for one hour so far,' he said, extending the index finger on his right hand.

'So, we hold out another finger each time it reaches 59:59?'

'Exactly, then to work out how long we've been running for, we just count up the fingers and then add on the minutes from the watch.'

'I love it,' I laughed. 'Genius idea.'

'Who needs hours on a stopwatch when you've got fingers.'

'What time is it, anyway?' I asked. 'We set off at 8.30am so it would be easier to just work it out from that.'

'I don't know. My watch says it's 4.38pm. I've never set the correct time on this watch.'

I burst out laughing.

'Oh my god! WHY? Telling the time is the ONLY other purpose that a watch has. It really is the most pointless watch in the entire world.'

'Just leave my watch alone. I like it.'

Mark likes his stopwatch so much that he accidentally left it at my house the following day when he got his train back to London. I did debate putting it in the bin and denying all knowledge of it, but I reluctantly posted it to him instead.

After several long and steep climbs and descents, the path then ambled down through the first wooded section of the course, with the mouth of the Kingsbridge estuary visible through the trees ahead. The path emerged above the beautiful beach at Sunny Cove, with the popular town of Salcombe sitting on the other side of the estuary from us. We had no idea of the mileage that we had covered so far, but guessed it to be under 10. It was a tremendous relief to reach the aid station at Mill Bay and discover that we had completed 11 of our 36 miles so far.

The aid station comprised of a watering can filled with water, and some Jelly Babies spread out on a small table. I reached for a Jelly Baby and discovered that it was sitting in a pool of water. It slowly disintegrated in my hand as I tried to pick it up, and the sliminess of it caused it to shoot from my fingers into the bushes behind. I didn't bother trying for another. Instead, we took a moment to refill our water bottles and eat some of our many provisions. I wasn't ready for the pork pie or pasty yet. We decided to treat ourselves to those later.

From Mill Bay, we followed a bridleway up the valley, sheltered on either side by trees. As we looped back round to the exposed coast path, the wind hit us hard again. This time, it was accompanied by the rain that had, until now, remained fairly innocuous. The conditions had deteriorated considerably.

Gara Rock is the site of a modern complex of holiday rentals, apartments, café, and spa facilities perched high on the cliff, with spectacular views in every direction. It was mid-morning and we gazed longingly through the café windows at tables full of people sitting in the warmth, drinking coffees and hot chocolates, and tucking into enormous slices of cake. They glanced at us through the window and then turned their heads quickly away, almost not wanting to witness our suffering in fear that it might taint the enjoyment of their comfort.

'We could always stop for a quick drink,' said Mark. 'It wouldn't be breaking any rules.'

'Do you think we'd ever be able to get up and come back outside again?'

'No, I think we'd be in there all day. That's still very tempting, though.'

We reluctantly carried on running.

After a very brief section of tarmac at Gara Rock, we rejoined the coast path, heading back towards Start Point the way we had come, this time with the sea on our right. We had not gone more than 50 metres when my feet slipped from beneath me on a grassy slope, and on this occasion I slid several metres down the hillside. Fortunately, we were away from the cliff edge, otherwise it could have had caused a very dramatic DNF to my life.

'You're making a bit of a habit of that,' said Mark, who had miraculously stayed upright so far. 'Are you alright?'

'Yes,' I said instinctively, climbing to my feet. It was then I realised there was a shooting pain in my left wrist. I must have landed awkwardly on it while using it to break my fall. It was very painful but felt like a sprain rather than anything too serious. And you don't need wrists to run, so I gritted my teeth and continued onward.

EIGHT

The route had doubled-back on itself for a mile or so and we crossed paths with some of the marathon runners coming the other way before our route turned inland. Things would be easy from then on. We were moving away from the exposed coast path, we would be sheltered in the valleys, the terrain would level out and the rest of the day would be a doddle. Or so we hoped.

We had not factored that the sandy, rocky terrain of the coast path had meant that, despite all the rain, the ground had been relatively dry in places. Inland, however, where the ground is soil-based, the mud was a different story. It made running with any style or finesse impossible. Not that I have ever run with any style or finesse, but those that did now looked like they were taking their first ever steps as humans. Running uphill felt like we were covering twice the distance, as our feet slid backwards with every forward stride. Running downhill involved a mixture of courage, skill and luck to try to remain standing, and running along the very few level sections of trail were a combination of both.

We had planned to eat on the uphill sections. Many of the hills were so steep and muddy that there was little point in trying to run up them, and it was often just as quick – and far easier – to turn the slow run into a brisk walk. Eating while walking seemed like a logical solution to save time. However, trying to eat and breathe while slogging up a hill was much tougher than we expected – particularly with the mud – and we crested each brow, feeling utterly exhausted. We were making ourselves eat at regular intervals, and although it was not a pleasant experience to force-feed ourselves, we did always notice a dramatic increase in our energy levels a few minutes after eating.

Most of the route so far had been inaccessible to spectators because of the remoteness. But as we reached the village of East Prawle at about the 14-mile point, it felt like a veritable metropolis; friends and families of runners standing in groups on the roadside, cheering as we passed. Not our own families, unfortunately. Mine had wisely stayed home in the warm and dry and Mark's were 300 miles away in Kent. But the energy and enthusiasm of the spectators on the roadside gave both of us a new lease of life and helped spur us on.

Soon after East Prawle, we joined a farm track across a muddy field, with deep tractor ruts overflowing with silky brown sludge. There was no way to gauge the depth of these pits until you stepped into them, and their size and frequency meant it was impossible to avoid all of them. It was simply a question of luck and hoping that the one you picked was less deep than the one you avoided. Occasionally, you would get lucky and the mud would just reach the top of your trainers – still just enough for the gritty soup to seep inside. Other times, you would plunge knee-deep into a seemingly bottomless pit and flail frantically as you heaved your submerged leg out of the stickiness, hoping that your shoe was at least still attached to your foot.

Several people fell here spectacularly. This section of the course also included the half-marathon runners, whose route so far had been relatively clean and easy compared to ours. Sprightly competitors would dash past us, with not a speck of mud on them above the ankle – some had somehow managed to even keep their shoes clean until this point. Not anymore. Many of the half-marathon runners were not wearing backpacks and could move quicker and more nimbly than us heavily laden ultrarunners. One young lady in bright turquoise shorts and a pristine white t-shirt skipped past me as I tried to prise my leg out of a bog. A few metres further on, she went to plant her right foot into what looked to me (and I assume to her) like a patch of relatively dry ground, considering. As her foot crunched through the crusty surface, her leg disappeared into the sludge below, swallowing her leg all the way up to her knee. The momentum of her energetic running caused the rest of her body to continue travelling forwards and she face planted straight into the next puddle. I somehow contained my laughter as she pulled herself up, every inch of her white t-shirt now covered in thick brown slime.

'Are you ok?' I asked.

'Yep, absolutely fine,' she said resolutely, a hint of laughter in her voice. 'I meant to do that.'

And off she skipped, albeit a little more gingerly than before.

NINE

At the far end of the field, we reached a bit of a bottleneck while runners waited to get through a gate into the next field. We shuffled slowly forwards through the mud and as we made it through the gateway, we could see what had caused the holdup.

A vast grass gully stretched out below us, with the field funnelling steeply down from both sides. Our route led straight down the middle. Judging by the speed at which runners were edging their way down the hillside, this looked to be the most treacherous ground we had encountered so far. Many runners were heading off to either side of the field, hoping to find some firmer ground before beginning their descent, while others inched slowly down the middle.

We watched a man in front of us take a tentative step down the hill before losing his footing completely. He fell on his backside and the gradient caused him to shoot down the hillside at a rapid speed for a good 20 metres before he brought himself to a stop.

'That looks awesome,' I said.

'Are you thinking what I'm thinking?' asked Mark.

'I sure am.'

There didn't appear to be anything too dangerous about the hill; we were inland, away from steep cliffs; there were no trees and no protruding rocks – at least, none that we could see. There was little point in wasting time edging our way down the field slowly, when inevitably, we would end up on our arses anyway. We might as well make the most of it.

'One, two, three, go!' I shouted, clutching my backpack straps tightly and running towards the top of the downslope. I took an enormous leap forward, swung both legs in front of me, and landed in a seated position. I was already travelling at some speed by the time I hit the muddy ground, and it only took a few seconds to reach what felt like terminal velocity. My shorts were sucked right up my bum crack, making it look like I was sledging in a thong. But it was so much better than sledging. Who needs snow? Or a sledge? This was the most fun I had had in ages.

I heard a whoop from Mark behind me and knew that he had also launched himself down the hillside. I must have travelled well over 50 metres before I heard a suspicious tearing noise from my shorts. Very few things could make running 36 miles in the conditions we had faced less appealing, but doing so with a pair of shredded shorts – and no underwear – would be a step too far. I tried in vain to dig my heels into the ground to slow me down, and I used the fingers on my right hand to scrape into the grass. My left hand was still sore after my fall earlier in the day, but I had temporarily forgotten about it until I was hurtling down a muddy hillside, unable to stop.

Eventually, after another 20 metres, I managed to bring myself to a stop. I was just climbing to my feet and in the process of trying to retrieve my shorts from up inside me when I heard a scream from Mark.

'WATCH OUT!' he shouted, as I dived out of his path, just as he whizzed by. He came to a stop a little further down the hillside and I walked down to meet him.

'That was amazing!' I said.

'It was brilliant. The highlight of the day so far.'

As we looked back up the hill, we could see dozens of people all following in our footsteps (or should I say 'bumslide prints'), power-sliding down the hill behind us. It was beautiful to watch.

'Well done, boys,' said one runner as he slid up alongside us. 'Looks like you've started a bit of a trend. I'm tempted to climb back up and have another go.'

'Are you sure this is the right way?' I asked Mark, half a mile further on.

'No, but this is where the sign pointed,' he said.

'But it's a river.'

'Maybe it used to be a footpath at some point.'

A torrent of water gushed down the narrow bridleway we were supposed to run up. To begin with, we tried to run on the grass to one side, but the grass was sporadic and the patches that we could find were marsh-like anyway. The only option was to run through the water.

I had forgotten what colour my trainers were, and it was a welcome sight to see the bright green return as the flowing water washed away the mud that had caked them for the past four hours (I know it was four hours because I counted the extended fingers on my right hand). We had also been joined on this section by the 10k runners, who had started several hours after us. There was a lively atmosphere as runners of all shapes, sizes, ages and abilities navigated their way upstream.

I initially felt strangely sorry for some of the 10k and half-marathon runners. Many of them would have been taking part in their first ever running event. They had signed up for a nice, scenic, coastal 10k in a beautiful part of the country. For those just getting into running, it would have sounded like a fine prospect. I could certainly see the appeal. But because of the brutal conditions, they had not quite got what they imagined. I wanted to stop and hug a couple of them and tell them, 'running events aren't usually like this. There's never usually this much rain, this much wind, or this much mud. Most races are on road and you don't have to worry about staying upright, and most of them are not nearly as hilly as this. Please don't be put off running events for life.'

But just as I was feeling sorry for them, I looked around and noticed that almost all the runners seemed to be having a brilliant time. There were constant squeals of glee and the sound of laughter. I mean, what was not to love? It brought out childlike qualities in all of us.

Running on tarmac is so dull when you can run through a torrent of muddy water instead. So I then went to the other extreme and felt like I should be commiserating with these first-timers and telling them to enjoy this as much as possible, because this would probably be the most fun they would ever have while running. It was certainly the most fun I had ever had while running.

TEN

After we reached the top of the stream, the half-marathoners and the 10k runners forked right by a sign that announced that they had '1 mile to go'. Part of me envied them; we still had about 18 miles to go. But I was feeling pretty good, and I was not yet ready for my run to end.

The runners thinned out considerably at this point, with just the marathoners and ultramarathoners remaining. We followed more waterlogged bridleways and footpaths – sorry 'trails' – and a section of minor road, which felt strangely surreal to have tarmac underfoot, before we emerged in the village of Stokenham. Passing a pub, a man (possibly the landlord), leaned against the doorway, smoking a cigarette.

'Why don't you call in for a pint?' he said.

'Don't tempt us,' I replied. 'We'd never leave.'

Mark was taking advantage of the level gradient and had picked up the pace a little. I did my best to keep up, but it felt uncomfortable. My breathing was laboured and my legs felt weak.

'Mark, I'm going to have to slow down a bit,' I called. 'Feel free to go off ahead, though. I don't want to hold you back.'

'Sorry, I probably was going a bit quickly. I was just a bit anxious about us missing the cut-off.'

'But we've got loads of time, haven't we? We're doing fine.'

'I thought the cut-off was at 3.15pm?'

'It is.'

'But it's about 1.30pm now. And we've still got over 12 miles to go.'

'But the cut-off time is not for the finish. It's for when we have to start our second smaller lap. Which is at about the 28-mile point. So we've got just under two hours to do about four miles. I think we will be alright.'

'Oh, thank god for that. Two hours for four miles? Wow, we could probably crawl that.'

'Yes! I wondered why you were suddenly running so quickly. Let's not crawl though.'

We reached Slapton Ley Nature Reserve, which was a part of the course I was vaguely familiar with. I had been here before on an organised bug hunt with my wife and children a couple of years previously. That is, the bug hunt was organised – we weren't hunting for organised bugs.

That day, the path had been dry, and the sun had been out. Conditions were a little different during the ultramarathon. The rain was teeming down and the path consisted of a gluey, boggy track dotted with deep puddles that couldn't be avoided. It certainly helped to slow Mark down.

We had been dreaming about the section of the route between the villages of Slapton and Torcross since about mile three. This section of road is one of the flattest sections of land in the entire South West. The road is distinctive because it sits on a thin spit of land, with the freshwater lake of Slapton Ley on one side and the saltwater of the English Channel on the other. It was going to be glorious. Just as our legs were beginning to suffer badly, our hard work would be rewarded with two wonderful miles of pancake flat pathway. And because of the sandiness of the soil by the sea, it was unlikely to be muddy.

'Just you wait,' I said to Mark. 'It's going to be bloody brilliant along that stretch. It'll feel like we are flying.'

We followed the road down from Slapton village to the coast road, where we realised instantly that things would not be as we hoped. We had been running through sheltered valleys and thick wooded areas for the past few miles, and now that we were back on the coast, we were reminded of one crucial element that had slipped our minds. The wind. With no hedges, trees or valleys for protection, this section was experiencing the full force of the weather.

We stopped briefly to fill our water bottles and chatted to an enthusiastic American who had flown all the way from California to take part in the event. Unlike Ricard, he embraced the conditions and was enjoying the day immensely.

'Oh my!' he shouted. 'What a day for a run! What a time to be alive.'

'Yes, the weather will definitely make the day more memorable,' said Mark.

'I picked this up from the airport on the way here yesterday,' he said, cracking open a can of something that he pulled from his rucksack.

'What is it?' I asked.

'It's a caramel fudge chocolate double espresso drink,' he said. 'Want some?'

'No thanks. Although it sounds pretty amazing.'

'WOO HOO!' he shouted, as he necked the lot and set off towards Torcross. 'Have a good one!'

'Thanks. You too.'

As we began running, the power of the elements became even more apparent. We were running directly into an almighty headwind, and it was incredibly draining to make any forward progress.

'You were right. It feels like we are flying,' said Mark. 'Just not in the direction we should be.'

'There's no point even running this bit,' I said.

'Well, it is flat.'

'Yes, but look, I can walk at the same pace that you are running.'

Bizarrely, it proved just as quick (or slow) to walk this section. Walking seemed to provide a more solid footing and enable us to push harder into the wind. There were two runners ahead of us in the distance who ran most of this section, and we didn't lose any ground on them over the two miles.

ELEVEN

The beach we were running alongside – Slapton Sands – was the location of one of the most tragic events in military history. In 1944, while preparing for the Normandy D-Day landings, Allied troops staged a large-scale rehearsal – known as Exercise Tiger – on the beach at Slapton. A series of catastrophic errors and a breakdown in communication between English and American troops contributed to the death of almost 1,000 soldiers. On the morning of April 27th, a friendly fire incident involving the Allied forces accidentally shelling their own soldiers on the beach caused the death of hundreds of servicemen. The following day, a three-mile long convoy of Allied boats taking part in the rehearsal was struck from behind by nine unsighted German E-boats, killing hundreds on board.

The incident was covered up for many years and it was not until a local hotelier – Ken Small – helped bring a sunken American Sherman tank to shore that any sort of memorial was built to mark the loss of life. This tank now sits in a car park near the village of Torcross, at the other end of the beach to Slapton.

Torcross has suffered badly in recent years at the hands of the sea. Many of the houses in the village sit in a line along the seafront, protected only by a sea wall. This wall has been breached several times over the years, but hopefully it won't be lost to the sea like Hallsands a couple of miles further down the coast.

From Torcross, we followed the coast path up and over a steep section of headland back down into the village of Beesands where the event began. Marathon runners would end their race here, and the ultrarunners would head out to do another smaller loop of about seven miles. Due to route logistics, the marathon course totalled 28 miles. So technically, that too was an ultramarathon.

As we ran along the road through Beesands, we saw four familiar faces up ahead. My wife Rachel, and my three children – Layla, Leo and Kitty – had all come to cheer us on. After seeing the weather forecast, I had tried my hardest to dissuade them all from coming, as I knew how grim it would be to spectate, and I wasn't able to predict – even to the nearest two hours – how long the race would take us.

But it was so great to see them all, and they had found a parking space right by the waterfront so had taken shelter in the car while they waited.

'Well done!' shouted Rachel as we staggered towards them. 'You both look really good. How does it feel having run 28 miles?'

'I think we both feel surprisingly good, considering,' I said to Mark, looking for confirmation.

'Yes, I feel much better than I thought I would. It's actually been great fun,' he said.

'I can't believe how jolly you both seem. It must be horrendous conditions to run in,' said Rachel.

'Yep, absolutely horrendous,' smiled Mark.

'Still fun though,' I added.

'You're doing much better than Daniel and Marta. They are giving up.'

'What? Are you serious? What do you mean they are giving up?' I said.

'They've had enough. They are only a few minutes ahead of you and they've decided that 28 miles is plenty for them and they're not going to do the other lap.'

'Really? Are they injured?'

'I don't think so. They just don't like it. They both looked really miserable.'

'What don't they like about it?' I asked, even though the answer was fairly obvious.

'All of it. The weather. The hills. The mud. They just looked really fed up. I've never seen them like that before.'

'If only we'd known they were so close we could have all run together.'

'Oh well,' said Rachel. 'I'm sure they'll be happier in the pub later.'

'That's true. Was Charles with them?'

'No, we haven't seen Charles at all. We've been here about 40 minutes and I'm fairly certain he hasn't passed us while we've been here.'

Mark and I both took huge handfuls of Jelly Babies from a box that Kitty was holding. She had quietly offered them to us, but kept the box extremely close to her chest, making it clear that although they were bought for us, she didn't actually want us to take any.

'We will hopefully see you in about an hour and a half,' I said. 'Thanks so much for coming to cheer us on. It's so lovely to see you all.'

'It's lovely to see you both do. Well done again. You've done brilliantly. Be careful out there.'

'We will.'

TWELVE

We followed the coast path out of the village of Beesands and then met the sign that directed marathon runners right, at which point they would funnel through into a field where the finish line was located. Those doing the ultra proceeded straight on. This would have been where Daniel and Marta forked right, and I felt a tremendous sense of disappointment for them. They must have both been suffering really badly to cut their race short.

With the marathon runners now off the course, we could see no other runners ahead or behind us. Only 99 runners started the ultramarathon, and the vast majority of these were way ahead of us, or even enjoying a mug of hot chocolate or a beer at the finish by now. The coast path felt extremely isolated, and I was very glad that Mark and I had stuck together. We still had about six miles to go, but it felt like we were almost there. We had covered 30 miles and our legs were at least still moving, albeit a lot slower than they had been earlier in the day.

We reached the village of Hallsands and I spotted a couple of people in the distance, climbing the steps on the other side of the bay. They both wore matching red jackets and identical backpacks.

'Look!' I said to Mark. 'Over there. Isn't that Daniel and Marta?'

'It definitely looks like them,' he said.

I tried to do a loud whistle, but all that came out of my mouth was a pathetic hiss and a load of crumbs and sticky spit from a bar I was midway through eating. I have never been very good at whistling and it proved to be an impossible task after running 30 miles, with a mouthful of food, into a gale-force wind.

'Daniel! Marta!' I shouted. To my delight, the two figures now at the top of the steps turned and began waving excitedly at us.

'Heeyyy!' they shouted, which is Spanish for 'Heeyyy'.

Mark and I crossed the beach and then panted up the steps to where they stood waiting for us at the top.

'Wow, are we glad to see you?' said Daniel. This was a rhetorical question. The happiness in his voice was obvious.

'Rachel told us you were stopping at the end of the marathon,' I said.

'Yes. We were.'

'But you're here, so you obviously didn't stop. What happened?'

'I don't know,' said Marta. 'We meant to stop, but we sort of just ran past the turning and ended up here.'

'How are you two still smiling?' asked Daniel. 'I don't understand.'

'It's been brilliant. Have you not enjoyed it?'

'No,' said Daniel resolutely. 'Brilliant? How was it brilliant?'

'It's just been really good fun,' I said. 'Have you not enjoyed any of it?'

'Nooooo! Absolutely not,' said Marta. 'It's been horrible.'

'But you ran a 100km race in the Pyrenees. And cycled 200km off-road on a mountain bike. Surely that must have been worse than this?'

'No. That was very tough, but at least it was dry.'

'And warm,' added Daniel.

'Have you really hated it all?' I asked.

'Every minute.'

'Did you get a bit hungry again, Daniel?' I said, remembering his rage near the end of one of our training runs. He laughed.

Daniel is the most enthusiastic person I have ever run with. He chats and smiles constantly and always makes running look effortless. He is more than happy to plod along at my pace, but gives the impression that he could always easily move up a gear if he wanted to. A couple of weeks before the ultra, I went on a long training run with Daniel, Marta and Charles. It was our first long trail run and my first ever run with a backpack. I quickly got used to the sensation of running with something on my back and it was reassuring knowing I had all that food so close at hand. I liked the idea so much that I considered carrying a backpack full of food wherever I go, even when walking around the house.

During that training run, we ran about nine miles along the coast path, and then turned around and began to run back. I started to struggle early on the way back. The hills were proving too much of a challenge, and I was really suffering. Charles seemed to speed up the longer we ran for. Marta looked like she was tiring a little, but Daniel, as always, looked in complete control.

We were less than a quarter of a mile from the end, and the sanctuary of the car, when I found myself running alone with Charles.

'What happened to Daniel and Marta?' he asked.

'I don't know. They were just here a second ago.'

We stopped and looked back down the coast the way we had come. There in the distance, we could see Daniel and Marta standing still in the middle of the coast path. We stood and watched for a couple of minutes and there was no suggestion that they were going to get moving in a hurry.

'What the hell are they doing?' said Charles.

'I've no idea. We are only about two minutes from the car.'

Eventually, they began running towards us and we waited to let them catch up.

'Everything alright?' I asked.

'Fine, fine,' said Marta.

'Yes, we're fine now,' said Daniel. 'I had a bit of a – how do you say in English? – melt... down back zere?'

'A meltdown? What happened?'

'I don't know. One minute I was fine and zee next my body decided to give up and I didn't want to run anymore.'

'A bit like Forest Gump?'

'Ha, yes, I suppose.'

'So what did you do?'

'He took all zee food that was in my backpack,' said Marta. 'He ad already eaten all heez.'

'What did you have?'

'Two energy gels and a chocolate bar. Zat is all she ad,' said Daniel. 'I wanted more.'

'TWO energy gels and a chocolate bar? Really? And we're only metres from the end?'

'I know, I know. I could not go any further. I needed to eat.'

It was the first time I had ever seen Daniel suffering, and it was reassuring to discover that he was human, too.

'So it happened again?' I asked. 'You got the hunger rage?'

'Yes, it happened again,' he laughed. 'But zis time not just for a few minutes. It 'appened for most of zee race.'

'Well, there's not much further to go. Shall we run the last few miles together?'

'Yes, we would like zat a lot. Thank you.'

THIRTEEN

We followed the same path along the coastline from Hallsands to Start Point that we had run along six hours previously. The ground was slightly wetter underfoot after several hundred runners had passed through, plus an entire day of rain. The wetter mud surprisingly felt less slippery than it had done on our first lap. Although, it is possible that our standards had changed after everything else we had experienced. It was still raining heavily, but we were relatively sheltered from the wind along this section.

All this changed when we reached the car park at Start Point. As we crested the hill, we experienced gusts of wind more powerful than I have ever felt in my life. Marta's slight frame was blown sideways into the wire fence to our left. I lost my balance too and held onto a wooden gate to keep myself upright. Mark and Daniel staggered backwards, holding on to each other to remain standing.

The route we were due to follow was the same treacherous stretch of coastline that we had followed early in the morning, up and down steep and rocky terrain, with sheer drops and a narrow path. It had been extremely tough going in the morning, but now the wind was significantly worse.

Just as we began to cross the car park to meet the start of the track down to the lighthouse, two race marshals in bright red coats and hats pulled down tightly over their heads dashed out from where they had been trying to seek shelter behind a small wooden hut.

'THIS WAY!' they shouted, pointing frantically to the road that exited the car park in the opposite direction.

'PARDON?' I shouted back.

'THIS WAY! We've had to change the route. It's too dangerous on the coast path down there.'

We were all huddled in tightly together next to the marshals and even though we were only inches away from them, it was still a struggle to hear what they were saying over the wind. They clarified that the conditions had deteriorated so much that the route had been altered and we would now follow an inland section instead.

I thought I would feel disappointed at the route being altered from the coast path to an extra inland section, but the fact that we could not stand upright in the car park made the idea of venturing back onto the exposed coast path seem foolish. The wind was so powerful that it made running in a straight line almost impossible. Running along the coast path could have proved fatal, and we were all secretly relieved to be on tarmac for a while.

And that's when the hail hit.

The ferocious wind that was battering us from the left side had brought with it its secret weapon. Tiny balls of ice (in case you don't know what hail is) peppered the bare skin of our faces, legs and arms. It felt like we were being whipped with nettles.

'It's times like this I bet you wonder why the hell you moved to England from Barcelona,' I shouted to Daniel and Marta.

'When we get to the finish line, we are driving straight to zee airport and moving back,' said Daniel, smiling as he pulled his hood tighter around his face.

We followed winding narrow roads and bridleways for a few miles before rejoining the original route.

'How can you both be smiling?' asked Marta.

'Because it's been a really fun day,' I said.

'I don't understand. Fun? How can you call today fun?'

'I don't know. The worse the conditions get, the more comical the whole thing is. I keep reminding myself that we paid money to put ourselves through this. I mean, how stupid is that? We actually PAID MONEY to suffer like this.'

'I know,' said Daniel. 'Don't remind me.'

'But that's what keeps me smiling. I can't blame anyone else, or feel sorry for myself. It was all my decision, and it's an experience I'll definitely never forget.'

'We won't forget it either. But not for zee same reasons as you,' laughed Daniel.

'How long have we been running for?' I asked Daniel.

'Six and a 'arf hours. Iz your watch not working?'

'I don't have a watch. Mark does, but it only goes up to 59 minutes and 59 seconds.'

Daniel burst out laughing.

'What appenz after zat?'

'It goes back to zero.'

'Don't be silly. Every stopwatch shows hours.'

'Mark's doesn't.'

'That's zee craziest zing I've ever 'eard. So you ave had no idea how long you've been running?'

'We held up fingers for the first few hours, but we lost count every time we fell over or stopped to eat.'

Daniel responded to this by nearly choking to death from laughter while trying to swallow an energy gel. It wouldn't have been a bad way to go.

Charles had run with Daniel and Marta for the first 20 miles, but then decided to run on ahead. He would be cosy and warm back in the car by now. The bastard.

'Are you glad you continued?' I asked.

'Yes, I suppose so,' said Daniel. 'It's great that we got to run wiz you two, but we would ave been perfectly appy to stop earlier.'

'Would you not have felt a little disappointed to get a Did Not Finish?'

'No, because 28 miles is still a veeeery long way and we just weren't enjoying it.'

'But you'll enjoy it even more later knowing you completed the full distance.'

'Maybe.'

'Charles is going to be annoying enough as it is after beating all of us. Imagine what he would be like if you didn't even finish the race?'

'That's true. I wouldn't 'ave been able to look at 'im ever again.'

We all agreed that anything that was considered a significant hill we would walk up. Walking proved to be not much slower than running, and was significantly kinder on the legs. As the race went on, our definition of what constituted a hill became a lot looser. At various stages during the final few miles, Daniel, Marta, Mark and I would debate whether a particular section of track or road was considered a hill. Often it was just the slightest of inclines, but all it took was for one of us to state categorically that it was a hill and we would all be allowed to reward ourselves with a brief walk.

The weather and terrain were so extreme it left us with very little time to think about how our legs were feeling. That is one of the benefits of trail-running – your mind is kept far more occupied that it would be along a road, so you focus less on the pain and suffering, and more on the experience.

We were nearing the finish and Mark and I still hadn't eaten our pork pie or steak pasty. We had run almost 36 miles in ridiculous conditions and made the experience tougher by carting around some heavy and impractical food items the entire way. We still couldn't face the idea of eating them, so decided to have them as a reward at the end. They were now squashed and soggy. What a reward that would be.

We met the flooded bridleway for the second time and trudged our way up through the rushing water, where we reached the '1 mile to go' sign again. This time we were able to fork right. This time I was ready.

FOURTEEN

As we crested a hill, we could see the marquees of the finish line. We had set off just after first light, the field filled predominately with the 99 ultrarunners. Since then, several hundred marathon runners, half-marathon runners and 10k runners had arrived, started their events, finished, and then headed home while we were still out on the course. The field in which we started and would finish was now completely deserted.

We ran up through the final gate and down towards the marquee – the door of which signified the finish line. The four of us crossed the line together in a time of 7 hours and 36 minutes.

The finish line was like none I have ever seen at an event before. It was an empty marquee sitting in several inches of mud. A lady emerged and congratulated us, then dipped our timing chips into a machine which printed off a paper slip with our finishing time. My paper slip had disintegrated in my muddy, wet hand before we reached the car. Another marshal handed us a medal, and then we retrieved our bags of dry clothes and headed for the car. It was certainly an anticlimax, but then no ending would have lived up to the day we'd had.

As we squelched our way out of the field, we met Rachel and the children squelching towards us.

'Have you finished already?' asked Rachel.

'Yes, just now.'

'Where was the finish line? I thought it was down here.'

'It was in that marquee, but you really didn't miss much.'

'Oh no, sorry. We were on our way there. Well done, all of you. You did brilliantly. How was it?'

Daniel and Marta looked at each other, shrugged, and laughed.

'It was amazing,' I said.

99 runners started the ultramarathon. Only 63 of us finished. I don't mean to suggest the other 36 are still out there somewhere, but they – like Ricard – called it a day for various reasons and were recorded as DNF on the race results. We were towards the last of those 63, but it didn't matter a bit. I was now, like Mark, officially an ultrarunner.

Running and I had never clicked. It was always hard. It always hurt. And it was always boring. Running the ultramarathon changed my outlook completely. Gone were the expectations of a finishing time. It didn't matter how long it took us. As ultra distances vary so greatly, and the terrain and the weather conditions have such enormous impacts on the speed, there is very little kudos given to a finishing time as it's so hard to compare from race to race. It's all about just getting to the end, one way or another, crossing that finishing line and never giving up.

I still don't know that I love running. But I did love the ultramarathon. Mostly because it involved a lot of time outside. And eating. Basically, I realised that I really love spending time outside. Whatever the weather. And I really love eating.

After training and competing in my first ever Ironman, I thought I was set on triathlon. I can't deny the excitement of mixing three very different disciplines, as it stops the mind from getting bored and keeps things interesting. But it's also quite a hassle. There is so much equipment involved in triathlon, and so many things that can go wrong. There's always a faster bike, better shoes, a sleeker wetsuit, more aerodynamic helmet, clearer goggles. Running felt extremely primitive in comparison. But in a good way. I love it for its beautiful simplicity. You can do it anywhere. You don't need any money. You don't need to check opening times. You don't need to remember your membership card. You don't need an opponent. You don't need to pump up your tyres or remember your goggles. You put on a pair of trainers, open your front door, and run – as far, and as fast or slowly as you like. That's really all there is to it.

Training for my Ironman, and now completing my first ultramarathon, had well and truly lit a fire inside of me. I was thriving on these new challenges and relished the thrill of pushing myself beyond my comfort zone. I wanted more. There were many other adventures I was already planning.

Part of what made the ultramarathon so fun, though, was being able to share the experience with Mark. It would have been very different on my own. Most of my previous runs and events had been undertaken solo and I had learned how much more enjoyable these challenges were with company.

Perhaps Rachel and I could run a marathon, or even an ultramarathon, together? Or maybe take part in a triathlon? Despite their misery, seeing Daniel and Marta competing together had got me excited about sharing these experiences with Rachel in the future. She had demonstrated no interest in trail running (or even footpath running, for that matter), and had shown no desire to take part in any cycling or swimming events either, let alone a triathlon. But she once had the same aversion to road running yet was now a certified running addict. It was definitely worth a try. Persuading her to join me could be my toughest challenge yet.

George Mahood

Chasing Trails

Author's note

Thank you for choosing to read my book. If you enjoyed it, I would be extremely grateful if you would consider posting a short review where you bought it and help spread the word about my books in any way you can.

You can get in touch via social media:
www.facebook.com/georgemahood
www.instagram.com/georgemahood
www.twitter.com/georgemahood

Or join my mailing list via my useless website to be the first to hear about new releases.
www.georgemahood.com
Signed copies of all of my books are available in my website's shop.

This ultramarathon was just the start.

Chasing Trails is the prequel to the DNF Series - a series of books about adventures with George Mahood and his family in running, cycling and swimming.

From ultramarathons to triathlons, 10km swims to European cycling adventures, George promises fun and laughter every step, pedal and paddle of the way.

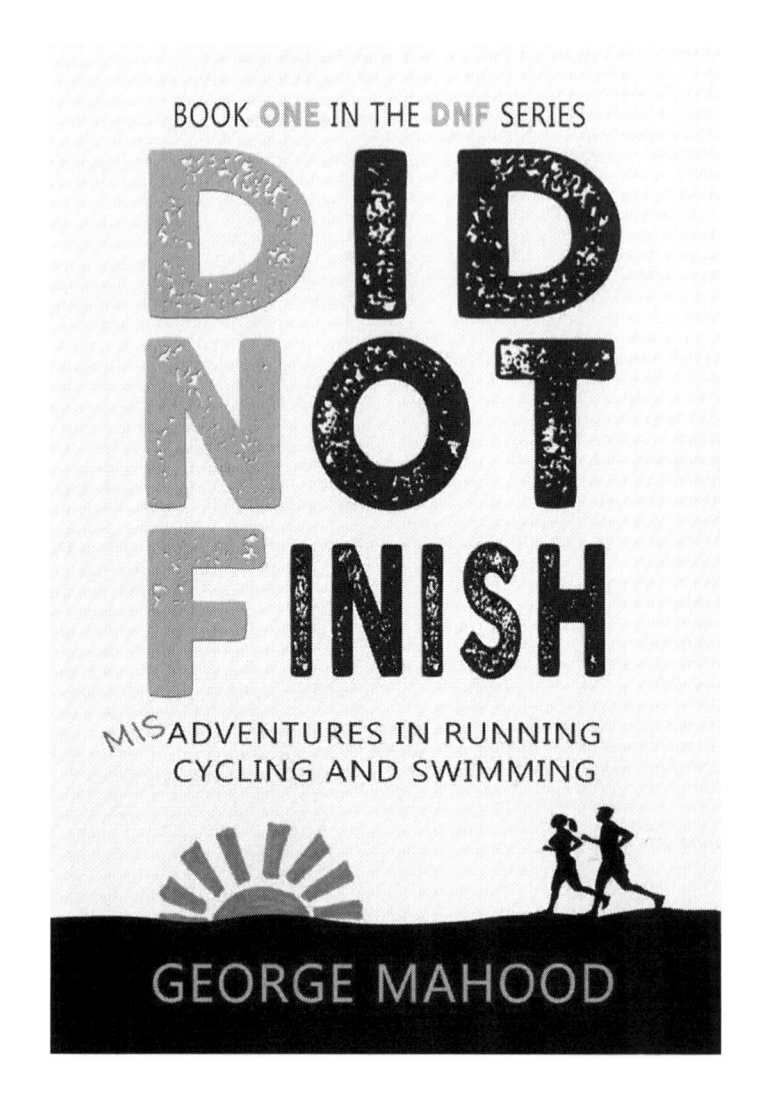

As well as the DNF Series, George has also written many other books. Please take a look...

Also by George Mahood

Free Country: A Penniless Adventure the Length of Britain
Every Day Is a Holiday
Life's a Beach
Operation Ironman: One Man's Four Month Journey from Hospital Bed to Ironman Triathlon
Not Tonight, Josephine: A Road Trip Through Small-Town America
Travels with Rachel: In Search of South America
How Not to Get Married: A no-nonsense guide to weddings… from a photographer who has seen it ALL

(all available in paperback, Kindle and audiobook)

Acknowledgements

Big thanks to Rachel, Tim Windram and Becky Beer for help with the editing of this book. Thanks to Mark for putting the idea of an ultramarathon in my head in the first place.

www.facebook.com/georgemahood
www.instagram.com/georgemahood
www.twitter.com/georgemahood
www.georgemahood.com